A BOOK OF COMFORT

Prayers for those
who walk in darkness

GRAHAM JEFFERY

First published in 1996 by
KEVIN MAYHEW LTD
Rattlesden
Bury St Edmunds
Suffolk IP30 0SZ

0 1 2 3 4 5 6 7 8 9

ISBN 0 86209 897 1
Catalogue No 1500068

Front Cover: *Refraction* by Hannibal Mane
(Private Collection). Reproduced by courtesy of
the Bridgeman Art Library, London

Typesetting by Vicky Brown
Printed and bound in Great Britain

CONTENTS

PREFACE

Perhaps the most appropriate moment of my ministry came during a visit to hospital, where I stopped to speak to a young woman on her own. And when it was time to go, and I thanked her for her company, she asked admiringly, 'Are you allowed out, then?' Which I was, as it happens, though all of us are locked into situations we cannot escape, and find ourselves being patients often enough, when we had hoped to be doctors.

These prayers then are written from the perspective of one who walks in the valley but hopes for the mountain top. They are for those who find life a burden, or sentence to be got through, rather than a gift to be enjoyed.

And since there is no easy medicine for the human condition, these prayers are offered with love, not so much to get us out of the pit as to help us find God in it. 'If I go down to hell, you are there also' (Psalm 139). Or, to use Graham Greene's adaptation of Jeremiah, 'and underneath are the everlasting arms, that this falling falling falling can't fall through'.

GRAHAM JEFFERY

Prayer

Lord, I am one of those on the ledge,
   and the ledge gets narrower over the
     years.
It has never been very wide
   but I have managed to live there;
   managed to survive,
   managed to smile.

My friends think I am doing rather well,
   things will somehow improve.
But the ledge is getting smaller
   until I have nowhere to stand.
Help me to cling on to your love,
   until I fall into your arms.

BEGINNINGS

This book is for those whose feelings of failure are greater than any feelings of success, who mow the lawn and see not the green strips of our life's achievement but the grass yet to be cut.

The prayers are in no particular order. They are like a recipe book to be dipped in and out of, hoping to find some phrase that may linger on the soul's palate. The first duty of love is not to do anyone any harm. And if these prayers achieve that, I am grateful indeed.

This book is written from the perspective of those who feel under condemnation, and have no sense of God's grace. And since words are of limited use, I have kept the text as brief as possible, limiting it to those stories or verses from Jesus' life which may be helpful.

The gospel of Jesus begins like a family occasion, with the birth of his cousin John, the nearest thing he had in this life to a big brother, or contemporary. Someone who did things before he did, like walking or preaching, and could show Jesus later how to do it.

And John's birth begins with his father calling him 'John': not 'Zacharias' after himself. We are all like that, in Zacharias' or Jesus' estimation of us. We are all ourselves with our own life and meaning. Each of us has our own name. And when we are unwell, Jesus thinks of us. 'This person has an illness': not 'this illness has a person'.

Jesus did not on the whole discuss reasons for our soul's illness, or discuss blame for the human condition. Forgiveness and kindness were his better treatment. Though he did on one occasion stand by our bedside while the doctors and specialists discussed the causes of a man's complaint. Some doctors said the condition was hereditary; others that the causes lay in the man's particular history. Jesus, when pressed, could only reply: this man became ill that I could help him. This woman became lonely, so God could be her friend.

1

Welcome to the rest of my life, Lord.
  The first day of it.
  It may be the only one.
  Were there other days?
  If so, you have forgiven them.
  Will there be other days to come?
  If so, they are your responsibility.
But here and now,
  I open the door and welcome you,
    friend of my darkest moments,
    friend in my despair.

2

I'm glad you are not a psychiatrist, Lord.
  Trying to understand me, unravel me,
  make sense of my life's complicated
      mechanisms.
You do more than understand me,
  you love me.
Reaching deep into my heart,
  you give me meaning.
No, I may not be 'normal'. Who is?
  No, I may not be 'balanced'.
  But I am myself,
  and in my complexities you love me.

3

You called us by name, Lord,
   before we called you.
Outside the tomb,
   in darkness of soul.
   In the failure of our lives
   you called us your rock,
     salt of the earth,
     light of the world,
     though we ourselves felt dark.
We were called Christians, Lord,
   before you were.
Jesus, my unknown friend, love me.

4

It is bad enough being a depressive without having the burden of religion to make it worse. Religion is the preserve of those who try to do better and so necessarily fail, and feel under condemnation.

But the attempt to do well is itself the chief glory and triumph. 'Well done, good and faithful servant', for trying and failing.

The best priests of Christians tend to be those who are older. They have failed most. People cling to Peter the first Pope (if he was that) because he was fallible. Not faultless.

5

For God has chosen us,
   the depressives of this world,
   to comfort the happy.
He has chosen us,
   who have no sense of our own value,
   to give other lives meaning.
He has chosen the lowly vessels
   to lift others high,
   the dirtied cups
   to wash and refresh others.
In my brokenness, Lord, I give you glory.

6

Help me to use the sufferings I've got,
   Lord.
I shan't, after all, be able to offer them to
   you forever.
   They are unique.
No one else has them, thankfully.
   No one else knows you
   in quite the way I do.
This burden is all my own.
   Yet all your own, always.

7

Do you take your life with or without wine?
   I suppose, Lord, we should do both.
   Accept the wine offered to us on our
        cross,
      any comfort, any blessing,
      any alleviation of our soul's pain.
   That which will help us bear our cross,
      be borne on it,
      no one else quite understanding.
   And yet in a way we cannot drink it.
   Our own life is our own gift, burden,
        terror.
Help us, dear Lord,
   to accept all the consolations life has
        to offer.
   But to decline that one consolation
      of stopping being ourselves,
      ceasing to be ourselves.
You love us, Lord.
You suffer with us, hold us up.

8

We are all in prison, Lord,
   of one sort or another,
   and no one knows,
   no one sees the bars,
      hemming me in,
         keeping life and opportunity out.
Nobody sees, Lord, except you.
You look at me as a father looks at his child,
   new born in a cruel world.
You keep watch over me,
   and release me, daily.

9

Now I see you, Lord, now I don't.
   Sometimes you are there, usually not.
And in darkness I go on,
   chiselling out my life painfully
   from this solid block of stone, so
         unyielding.
I chip away slowly, Lord.
A pattern slowly emerges.
   Not seen until the end.
One day you will see the finished work,
   and be well satisfied with it.

10

This prayer, Lord, is for those who find
    life a handicap.
  A burden, not an opportunity.
  A sentence to be endured,
  a day to be got through somehow.
Please bless my handicap, Lord.
  I may be doing better than I know.
Please bless my burden.
  I may be carrying more than I realise.

11

No doubt you love me, Lord,
  but I cannot experience your love.
No doubt the sun shines,
  but it does not warm my soul.
The rain falls,
  but does not refresh those deep parts
    of me
  only your brokenness can touch.
So I cling to your cross, Lord,
  though I'd rather have your resurrection.

12

Any book of prayers has its disadvantages. None more so than a book of prayers by a priest. For religion is meant to be comfort to us, and not judgement. Consolation when it cannot be inspiration. Religious people, though, tend to be those who try harder. And so fail more than others, because they are aiming high. 'Those who would serve God best are most conscious of wrong within.'

I hope this book is not seen as judgement. But consolation only. God beside us in the pit, as the long day wanes, and the sun begins to fall in the sky.

I hope you will still believe in the value of your life, though you cannot sense it. And pray for me a sinner.

13

Help me to use the sins I have, Lord.
I won't get the chance
    to fail in this way again.
    And if I do, I'll be older,
        more grateful for your forgiveness.

14

It says in the book, Lord, that you love me.
But I do not experience this love,
   have no feeling of it.
Other people ask, 'How are you?'
And I am not able to answer.
Dully, and in pain, I go on slowly.
Like you, I find the wine offered on my
       cross cannot help.
For I am totally alone.
And yet, on the way to my cross,
   I accept such solaces as the world
      affords.
Weep for the world, Lord.
   And, in your mercy, save us.

15

Stop the world, Lord
   I want to get on.
Breathe again my first breath.
   Start again my first steps.
Hear again the first words ever said to me.
   Son, daughter,
     I love you.

16

I wish I was dead, Lord.
  But this is not strictly true.
I wish my sufferings were dead,
  I wish the blackness of my mind
      would disperse.
But since it has not dispersed,
  I keep my hand in the hand of one
      I cannot feel,
  and thank you that I have managed
      thus far.
And do I wish I was dead?
  Say, rather, I wish I was alive.

17

I do not ask to be filled with wine, Lord.
  Ordinary water will be enough.
Though I long sometimes for a more
      visible discipleship,
  a more obvious way of serving you.
And yet,
  being filled with this plain water, Lord,
  I only ask that you pass your hand over it,
  changing its contents,
  with all their inadequacy,
  into your wine.

18

Dear Lord, I will carry any cross you like,
    provided it is not my own.
I find my own weaknesses so hard to bear;
    my own failure;
    my own depression.
And yet, as well as I may, I offer my life
        to you.
I ask you to bless it if you can,
    in ways I may never know.
I ask you to use my failure, my breakdown,
    to help others in their quest for faith.
Dear Lord, I offer my life and my failures
        to you,
    to be a blessing for others.
In your way and in your time,
    please use me, for Jesus' sake.

FOR COMFORT'S SAKE

Though Jesus of Nazareth was not a doctor, those who met him tended to feel better, whatever their age. His friendship was his treatment. And those who only touched the outskirts of his life found themselves standing straighter and taller than before.

St Luke, himself a medical man, gives us the most personal gospel. And, being a doctor, he knew the value of family ties and upbringing in Jesus' own life. He begins his own gospel with the family then, Jesus' aunt and uncle, Elizabeth and Zacharias. And how they named their own child John (the baptist), though no one in their family had had that name before. None of us, they were saying, is a recycled edition of his parents. We all have our own unique name and meaning.

So Jesus welcomes us to this new day. We are ourselves, and quite unique in God's perception of us. Our sufferings and experiences and triumphs are unique also.

19

I change houses, Lord, but never my
    home.
My true home is in your word daily, your
    love.
I change jobs, but never that one work
    of chiselling away at your likeness.
I change friends.
    Imperceptibly they drift away,
    faces mingle in the crowd,
        disappear, reappear.
But you are always there, smiling.

20

Listen to my words, Lord.
    Especially those I am too shy to utter,
        even to myself.
Listen to my hopes,
    even those I never knew I had.
Listen to my fears,
    those I cannot describe,
        only experience.
Above all, Lord,
    beneath all this,
        listen to me.

21

You set me at liberty, Lord.
  You give me freedom.
Touch the deep parts of my soul,
  unleash new energies,
  new possibilities,
  new worlds for my soul to visit.
And yet I live in one world only.
  Your world.
  Your kingdom.
Slowly it changes,
  or I change in it.
You lead me to new countries,
  beyond the map.

22

You turn water into wine, Lord.
Most people seem to turn wine back into
      water.
The world takes my best endeavours,
  my attempts at goodness,
  and belittles them,
      makes small of them.
But you magnify my virtues,

make great my littleness.
Stretching out your hand
over the ordinariness of this day,
    you bless it.
    You bless me.

23

Here I stand, Lord, with a world to be fed.
My two hands held up to you,
    five fingers on each.
My two loaves and five fishes,
    all I have with a world to be fed.
But you take my contribution to the
        world's need.
    You hold it high, hold me high.
    You give thanks for my life,
        and my actions this day.
However small, they travel outward
    till the world is fed.

24

When I was a child,
　　I thought as a child,
　　spoke as a child.
But when I grew up in your word,
　　the world got stuck to my fingers.
But I never lost my childhood, Lord,
　　so far as you are concerned.
Wherever I go, whatever happens,
　　I am still your little one,
　　the servant you delight in.

25

Help me to keep my eyes, Lord, on the
　　　road in front.
Yes, I have to check in the rear mirror.
　　Where I have been is important.
　　It led me to where I am now.
There are always cars trying to overtake,
　　those whose lives have more
　　　horsepower,
　　whose feet are constantly on the pedal.
And yes, there are always those
　　who will be ahead of me, faster.
But, such as I am, I am coming.

26

You bless our mistakes, Lord, as well as
  our virtues.
Sometimes our mistakes are the best part
  of us.
  Leading us to positions from which
  your love can rescue us,
  enable us, assist us,
  in a new way.
Help me to do my best, Lord.
  But not better than my best.
Help me not to push the issue,
  or my health,
  further than they can go.
It's your world, Lord.
  Your responsibility.
Don't rub out my mistakes.
  Weave them in.

27

You see the life I try to live,
  inside the life I live.
You take me to new pastures.
  Enable me to gallop.

Discover new parts of my soul
    I never knew existed.
I was happy in that ignorance!
But now I am older, Lord,
    and if I don't feel wiser,
    you at least never leave me.
You touch those parts of me
    other prophets cannot reach.

28

You are my defender, Lord.
You lift up my head,
    and pour in oil and wine
    to those deep wounds life has left.
Your water cleanses me.
You set me on your own beast.
You walk beside me to the inn.
You help me walk again,
    in my own time,
    at my own pace.
The future belongs to you also.

29

My other car is a Jaguar, Lord.
  My other dog a Rottweiler.
  My other wife or husband a film star.
But you are concerned with the life I
  have, Lord,
  this day ahead of me,
  this moment now.
You specialise in the actual,
  as well as the impossible.
You are the God of those whose feet are
  caked in mud,
  while their heads are in the skies.

30

The world is my oyster, Lord,
  and not my hospital.
And if it is my hospital
  I get out of bed while no one is looking.
  And in spirit at least
    move nearer the door.
You are my visitor, at all hours,
  not only those appointed.
My doctor on call, constantly.
My strength, my hope, my friend.

31

I never was any good at heights, Lord.
  Looking down from the theologians'
      lofty position.
  The angels' position, who give you glory.
I am more at home at the crib,
  looking over the wooden edges.
I notice amid the straw,
  the ox and ass gazing at me.
  Expecting great things.
  They still do.
You are very particular who you visit, Lord.
  You visit me.

32

I love my wife, Lord,
  though I am not married.
My brother and sister,
  though I am an only child.
My mother and father,
  though they left home years ago.
The world is your family, Lord.
This one person I meet today
  belongs to me also.
  I am never alone.

33

It's not that I worry more, Lord.
Just that I have more to worry with.
   More years, more failures, more bruises.
   These I carry with me.
   They are my scars, my battle medals,
      worn by me unwillingly for you,
      who worry about me!

34

It takes twenty-two years to be
      twenty-two, Lord.
   You can't hurry it.
Pull at the flowers in your garden
   to make them grow faster,
      us grow faster.
One day I'll outgrow the wayward
      impulses of youth.
   Move over to the middle lane,
   then the slow one,
   on life's motorway.
One day I'll stop altogether.
   Get out and enjoy the view, your view.
Till then, at my own speed, I journey
   onward.

35

My heart is fixed, Lord.
And no, I've not got arthritis.
My heart is rooted only
    in a love that never changes,
    a faith in me that never alters,
    a hope for my future
        as well as my past,
    that both may be blest.
My hope is in you only, Lord.
My faith and love are in you alone.
My heart is rooted and grounded
        in your love.

36

I possess the world, Lord,
    its farthest places.
Though I am confined
    to one small life,
    one particular moment
    in the world's time.
Yet my spirit soars.
    Beneath my frail body,

beneath the burdens of my soul,
beneath my mind, even,
you are there.
You never leave me.

37

Though I am born outside society
    you come to me in my stable.
Though my life is not accepted
    in the synagogue or the inn,
    still you watch over me
        and are my friend.
Though I die on the cross,
    condemned by all the gods,
    and all the doors of society
    remain closed to my presence,
and though I am buried in a borrowed
        tomb,
    with no chance of ceremony,
    still you wait with me,
    and send angels to roll back the stone.
You say I am alive.

DAY BY DAY

The chief difficulty for religious people is not whether God exists, but whether we do. Jesus affirmed the value of each person he met, finding faith in the most unexpected places. He did not go about saying, 'I am the Christ', but helped other people to feel they were.

Zacchaeus was so small he had to climb a tree to feel ten feet tall. Mary of Magdala was given her name back, and known by her name 'Mary', not by her town or supposed occupation.

But what if Zacchaeus climbed his tree because Jesus was a small man and got lost in the crowds? We are not given any indication of Jesus' appearance or habits, only those of his cousin John. But Jesus may have been a small man in one way. Like all prophets and healers he looked up to other people and made them feel taller.

As he does to us today. Looking at us and smiling and saying: Great is our faith.

38

Dear Lord, day by day you name me,
   give my life meaning.
There will never be another 'me'
   in all history.
The circumstances of my life may be
     common,
   may be depressed.
But I am of such value to you, Lord.
You begin your gospel
   with your own personal shepherd
   checking things out, to make sure I
     am safe.
While Caesar is saying, 'Count everybody',
   you are looking at me and saying,
   'Everybody counts'.

39

Dear Lord, you are my God.
Early will I seek you.
   My soul waits on you,
   to do your work in me today.
I bless you in the morning.

40

It's all right, Lord,
   I'll let myself out.
Day by day I say this,
   longing to be released
   from a life that is no life,
   from a life that has become
      seeming death and absolute pain.
And yet I carry on, Lord.
Linger here for a moment only.
   This moment is enough.
   And if I can bear this moment,
      I look no further.

41

Is there a life before death, Lord?
   That's what I am worried about.
   The next world can wait till I get there.
   One world at a time,
   one day at a time.
And yes, I know there will be a better
      tomorrow.
   Nothing good can ever be lost.
But I'd like to have the comfort of this
      morrow,
   around me today.

42

Lord, I offer you my sins.
Anyone can be a success,
  it depends what you are successful at.
But it takes real skill to be a failure.
  Absolute skill to be a disaster.
But you managed it,
  in that one moment of time,
  utter dereliction,
  no comfort from man or God at all.
You said, 'It is finished. It is complete.'
You touched me,
  in my own dereliction.

43

If I go up to heaven, you are there.
If I go down to hell, depression's darkest
    pit,
  you are there also.
You never leave me.
  You sustain me.
  And if you cannot rescue,
    you always love me.
  Your arms around me for eternity.

44

Keep me away from the pit, Lord.
One more day eked out of life's prison
    sentence,
  so many years to do,
  when even a fortnight would be enough.
Though it may become also
  a chance to meet you,
  to know you
  and to share at the end
    my sense of nothingness,
    my loss of identity.

45

It is hard to love you, Lord,
  hard to be certain of your presence.
Yet you are with me, you love me.
And, if I am uncertain of my own response,
  I know my uncertainty is your gift also,
  as in the gospel, so now,
  you stand at my door and knock.

46

You know the secrets of my heart.
You know that I love you.
Deep down beneath my sins
   and ingrained habits of wrong and
         failure,
      you see the true me.
You love me. You are my friend.

47

The sea is so large, Lord.
   My boat is so small.
I set out, with the deeps beneath me,
   and the far horizon farther
   than I can travel to, or even imagine.
   And yet, as well as I may, I am coming.
Using the winds given,
   even though they are all against me,
   and all I can do is veer sideways,
   nearer your kingdom, my destination.

48

I do not cry to you out of the pit.
I do not raise my voice.
    There is no need.
No need to shout,
    only to whisper quietly in my heart,
    that I need you.
    And find you,
    here in the muddy clay,
        beside me.

49

Help me to close that door.
It hangs open, swinging on its hinges.
I did not go that way,
    take that path, that job, that preferment,
        that wife or husband.
Help me to live in the now, Lord.
    Not in the might-have-been.
Help me to live in the present now.

50

The saddest words in Shakespeare are 'Othello's occupation gone'. And the saddest words in Jesus' parables may have been those of the labourers waiting in the market-place: 'No one has hired us.'

Jesus always hires us and has work for us to do. Even when that work is only trying to be ourselves.

He found Peter and Andrew fishermen, and turned them into prophets. He found Matthew a tax collector, and gave him employment in another currency. So he finds us today and asks if we will serve him. Even if we cannot do much, and are a 'patient', having things done to us, instead of doing them ourselves.

We are always irreplaceable to God, and serve him even when we do (or seem to do) nothing. Jesus loves us when we are in pyjamas.

51

I find this day a burden,
　　this moment a burden.
And yet it is, no doubt, your gift also to me.
　　A thing given,
　　though you yourself only want to give
　　　　me life,
　　　　not death.
The depression, the darkness
　　is a thing you do not wish for me,
　　but somehow have to allow.
Help me to remember, Lord,
　　the state of the world is not my fault.
The state of my own world,
　　so isolated and restricting,
　　is even less my fault.
You love me in this disability,
　　this slow awkwardness.
You are with me in it, underneath me,
　　not above me offering exhortations.
Lord, if I can bear it,
　　I'll get out of bed.

52

Help me to get out of bed, Lord.
It is such a long way to the ground.
Astronauts land on the moon,
    but I have this difficult task
    of re-entry into this world's atmosphere.
My world's atmosphere,
    my own world, so alienated, so alone,
    and only I know what it is like to be me.
Yet you know me, Lord.
    You love me.
    You give me my name,
    day by day, hour by hour.
You name the parts of your rifle, each
       morning.
    The parts of your church, your kingdom.
It's a long way to the ground, Lord.
    Help me.

53

Have you a miracle left over, Lord?
Me, for whom every day is a miracle,
    if I can endure it.
    If you can endure it, in me.
    Bring me through it.

Keep me company, in your own apparent
    absence.
    Lord, save me.
    Lord, save the world.
Begin with me, Lord,
    in your own unhurried time,
    at my pace.
        Not the world's.

54

One day at a time, Lord,
    has always been your policy.
    One hour at a time, this moment now.
Evensong seems a long way off.
    Supper is a distant Matterhorn
        waiting to be climbed.
But this moment, Lord,
    holds all my past memories and
        friends.
    By breathing in now, I love them, am
        with them.
    In breathing out, I offer you my love.

55

Tea-time, Lord.
I never thought I would get this far,
    but I have, or rather you have.
    And so, by your grace,
        I give you glory
        by being here, not by doing.
Like Alfred J. Prufrock,
    I measure out my life in coffee spoons.
    Each one such an achievement.
    A candle burning on the poor altar of
        my love for you.

56

It's a nice day, everyone says.
    The sun is shining.
    And yet it's not a nice day in my head.
    Anything but.
    Deep cloud banks of depression,
        constant dark.
And yet at least, Lord,
    in you I have one person
    who does not say 'be sunny'.

You are sunny, only in your kindness
    toward me,
  this disposition, this constant attitude.
You love me.
    In tight cloud banks of grey,
        you pray for water to collect and
           break.

57

Lord, please tell me who I am.
I have changed job,
  been divorced,
  lost my house,
  lost any sense of identity or direction.
Yet you tell me who I am.
Only love can reach certain conditions:
  only you on the cross.
Love is the answer.
    What was the question?

COMING ABOARD

Life is hard enough, without being told we should enjoy it. And Jesus did not spend his life telling the crowds to 'have faith'. He spent his life among people, trying to give it to them. 'Not menus but food' was always his response to our needs. As it is today.

He stands before us with his two hands and five fingers on each. Two fishes and five small loaves, all any of us are issued with for life's picnic. And Jesus says to us, somehow, hesitantly, not proudly, 'It is enough'. The five loaves and two small fish: the inadequate things or circumstances of our own life are somehow enough to feed the world.

None of us knows the value of our own life. Especially when we seem to do nothing. 'Whoever saves (or feeds) one soul, it is as if he had saved the whole world.'

58

The chess board of my life is
    complicated, Lord.
  Hemmed in on every side,
  in check perpetually,
  by those stronger pieces
  I can never match or remove.
And yet, Lord, weak positions have their
    grace also.
  Weak pieces, moved by your hand,
  can advance the kingdom in ways no
    one can foresee.

59

You give me faith, Lord,
  not in myself, but in my weakness.
  The inabilities of my life
    are places you can visit.
  The empty pages, places where you
    can write.
Morning by morning you waken me,
  and touch my ear.
  That I may speak to those who are
    weary,
    a word in season.

60

Release me for service, Lord.
These chains of my own life
   (no doubt I fastened them)
   which hold me fixed
      to this limitation, this circumstance.
I am married to my inabilities, Lord.
   What would I do without them?
Help me to remember, Lord,
   as the chains thicken,
   that I am your ambassador in chains.
Yes, I do wish I was a roving ambassador.
   But in my cell, you come to me.

61

Give me back my future, Lord.
   Or, if that is a diminishing asset,
   give me back my past.
But when that fades also, Lord,
   becoming blurred, inaccessible,
   give me, I ask you, this moment only.

62

The cross, Lord,
    is your ultimate status symbol.
    Not the resurrection.
But this inability on your part,
    this failure to move,
    is that which conditions me to your love.
Inability on your part,
    ability on mine,
    to see at last what you are in the world.

63

Give me faith, Lord.
    Not in you, but in myself.
    Your life in mine.
Give me hope,
        not that you will act well.
You have no option.
    But that I will.
Give me love, not for you, Lord.
    You have enough already.
But give me love, just a little,
    for my own poverty.
Help me to say, 'Well done'.

64

Do you remember the burning bush,
    Lord?
Other people saw a mass of disfigured
    branches,
    dried leaves in need of water.
    As I am, dying of neglect, in apparent
    plenty.
Starved of love, though surrounded by
    people.
But you see the sunlight through the
    branches.
    You see light in my life.
    Possibility, shining.
You take off your shoes, Lord,
    and enter my life humbly.
To others a sinner,
    to you I am your friend.

65

It does not matter
    if I don't believe in you, Lord.
    You believe in me.
It does not matter
    if I have no sense of your presence.

You have sense of mine.
  Are mine.
  Breath as I breathe.
  Feet as I walk.
Closer than my heart, you love me,
  and are my friend.

66

Jesus was known as the friend of publicans and
sinners, and was put to death, as love always is,
by 'the system' or establishment. He died
without any human consolation, apart from
the prayers of two or three friends. He had no
religious consolation. No sense of triumph for
himself in any after-life, though he gave
comfort as best he could to the two patients in
the beds either side of him, in life's emergency
ward. Only one of them listened. And Jesus' cry
of dereliction still haunts us: 'My God, my God,
why have you forsaken me?' And yet this 'at-one-
ment' is seen later as the moment our human
condition touched solid ground. Ultimate
reality: or perhaps un-reality. The state of not
being, of not being able to believe anything.

Should we experience this, may God bless

us. Not in the heavens above. But in our own
broken heart and mind. This is God's dwelling
place and home. 'If I go down to hell, God is
there also.'

67

Help me to forgive myself, Lord,
   as well as other people.
Help me to know the sun is put there
   to shine on me,
   the rain to wash and refresh.
You don't keep an eye on me, Lord.
   You keep both your eyes and all your
      heart,
    on me, around me.
You are greater than my heart.
   You know all things.
When I hold up my hands
   and say, 'It's my fault, I am to blame',
   you thank me, but also add,
   'Don't take all the blame for yourself,
     child,
    I need some of it myself'.
Help me to use my sins, Lord.
Help me to love you as I am, first of all.
   No more is needed.

68

Help me to be easy with myself, Lord,
     patient, kind.
I am not a wheelbarrow, needing to be
     pushed.
   But a child, needing to be loved,
        coaxed into virtue.
Help me to appreciate the flowers in my
     garden.
They won't grow any quicker
   by being criticised.
They need the constant rain and warm
     sunshine
   of your love, your approval.
Shine on me, Lord.
It's your job to do so.

69

Thank you for not telling me to cheer
     up, Lord.
   The world is hard enough
   without having to enjoy ourselves.
Thank you for not telling me 'not to
     worry';

I tried once not to worry,
    but failed.
I ended up worrying because I was
      worrying.
But you break these ever-decreasing
    circles,
    break the endless cycle
    of guilt engendering effort,
    engendering failure,
    engendering more guilt.
Put simply, you love me.

70

I have an eye on the clock, Lord.
    But two feet on the ground are better.
Help me to do those earthly things
    that bring me blessing.
Take whatever blessings life offers.
Life passes away, Lord,
    as I read these words,
    live this moment.
    Help me, quietly,
    return it to you.

71

Help me to look at the sun, Lord.
I, who do not feel the warmth of the sun,
   hope it shines on others.
In the darkness you love me, Lord.
   Come to me, across the waters
   of my own failures.
In the sunshine, though I do not feel
      your warmth,
   you share my dereliction.

72

I sing of what I want to believe, Lord,
   or would do, if I had better voice,
   and better heart.
Help me to remember
   as I go about my tasks;
   not too many,
   for then I'd get tired;
   not too few,
   for then my mind would over-race my
      body.
Help me to remember this only
   in the darkness:
      you believe in me.

73

Are you there, Lord?
If so, you're keeping remarkably quiet.
Can you not come to me in this
        breakdown,
    when I have no sense of your presence
    and maybe, never have.
Help me to remember, Lord,
    you are with me when I don't feel you.
    Especially then
    your own experience of the human
        condition
    speaks to me.
        Forsaken. But why?
    No comfort at all,
    the tree devoid utterly of any leaves.
Except this bare truth that you love me
        in my nakedness,
    all virtues or social occasions stripped
        away.
        You love me to the end.

74

Thank you for taking my 'breakdown'
    seriously, Lord,
  but for laughing also
  at things we can laugh at together.
Thank you for loving me,
  not trying to hurry me,
  not trying to make me 'normal',
  crank me up.
Thank you for seeing me behind my
    condition.
You take my illness seriously,
  but me more seriously still.

75

Listen to what I say, Lord.
  Not what I am.
  Do what I ask, Lord.
My requests are always better than my life.
  My alleluias sound well,
  my life sounds ill at ease,
    and out of tune.
But you love your sparrows, Lord,
  your crows as well as your nightingales.
And knowing this,
    I praise you in the morning.

76

Thank you for coming to my funeral,
    Lord.
  Not the hymns and eulogies,
  the prayers and pauses,
  the coffin's slow carrying in and out.
But thank you for coming to me,
  receiving me, lifting me up.
Thank you for coming to my resurrection.

77

Thank you for my insecurity, Lord.
  What would I do or be without it?
I should be insufferable in my success,
  and list of things achieved.
But I have only one achievement, Lord,
  of knowing that you love me.
And this one person I shall meet today.
Whoever blesses one person,
  it is as if he has blessed the whole world.
I'm ready to bless the world, Lord,
  with this weakness
    you have allowed me.

78

Some people are eagles, Lord.
   Able to fly at the sun direct.
      See their ways.
      Feel their purposes.
But I am one of your sparrows, Lord.
The smallest coins in human currency.
   Sold for a farthing.
   Two small doves,
   the price your servants paid
      for Jesus' birth.
Eight days old at the temple,
   another Jew, another poor citizen.
And yet I am not poor, Lord.
   Caged, waiting to be offered.
   Free in my own limited way,
      I stretch out my wings, and fly.

79

Help me to take the tablets, Lord.
Not to let me out, finally,
   but help me to endure
      one day
      one moment
      at a time.

80

Those who follow Jesus in darkness do a
great work. The wise men followed the star to
Bethlehem, which comforted them. But they
went home in darkness, by an unfamiliar route,
that Jesus might live and grow in safety.

We who follow Jesus in darkness also help
him to live, in others.

81

Is this what they call the 'dark night of
    the soul'?
In that case, Lord, I'd have preferred the
    early evening.
I understand now why five thousand
    turned up to your picnic
  but only three to your crucifixion.
You got it wrong, Lord,
  or perhaps we did.
Perhaps the five loaves and two small fish
    were on Good Friday also
    your chief congregation.
Two or three at the Cross's foot,
    a small congregation.

All I may see today in my bed-sitting
    room of a life.
  But you are there with us,
  helping us to feed a whole world.

82

Don't take my mind to bits, Lord,
  it's been dismantled enough already.
  Taxed beyond endurance,
  its parts strained and broken,
  its fuses blown.
But you loved me, Lord,
  when I was a baby and could do
      nothing.
You'll love me when I'm old and senile,
  if I get so far,
  and can do nothing again.
I don't need to justify myself to you, Lord.
  You are in me already, doing just that.
But give me one simple task, Lord,
  one simpleness of visit or letter I can do.
May I find rest and re-creation in that.

83

When I am weak, Lord, then I am strong.
When I have nothing left,
    except this present moment of
        weakness,
    you come to me, bless me,
    are well satisfied with your creation,
    and still say,
    'I have done all things well'.

84

Water is a good thing to walk on, Lord,
    though it leaves no apparent footprints.
Dry land is so much harder.
These fluid situations, these fragile
    circumstances
    that will bear no weight at all,
        except love's weight
    which is no burden.
Come to me, walking over the water.
Those situations that will not bear
    examination,
    only bring me closer to you.

85

We have no record, Lord,
  of how much you did,
  how often you got into Peter's boat,
  how loudly you spoke.
Only how you lived,
  how you spoke,
  that you loved me well,
  and made all things,
  your life especially,
  for my sake.

86

You are greater than my heart, Lord,
  You know all things.
  You forgive all things.
  You bear all things.
  You keep no score of wrongs,
  only of my attempts or wishes to serve
    you better,
    know you, love you, walk beside you
    in the darkness.
Shine, Lord, where you can.

87

Don't be hard on yourself, son.
Don't judge yourself so harshly, daughter.
   God is my father and mother rolled
       into one.
   He is the one who dies for me daily.
   He looks beneath my sins,
     to see his son, his daughter.
   He sees what I am now,
     and shall be later, in eternity.

88

Out of the deep have I called to you.
   Out of the tomb,
   out of the sepulchre.
Bandages wrapped round, securing me
    firmly.
   No chance of escape,
   but you call me through the bandages.
I cannot alter life's complications.
You call me through the grave-clothes,
   and one day will roll back the stone.

89

I cling to the wreckage, Lord,
   though I would rather be
   sitting in the boat,
   steering it,
   helping you to.
But perhaps I am in the boat, Lord.

Your family,
   your boat,
   so frail in
   its human condition.
Peter and Andrew, pray for me.
James and John, lower your nets.
I'm not coming aboard,
   but am with you already.

90

It's all a pretence, Lord,
   these prayers I say,
   this attitude I put on.
I don't feel it,
   do not feel anything,

only emptiness,
the dark side of the soul.
But one day
I shall by your grace,
and my patience, wake up
after your likeness.
And be
well satisfied.

Deep Waters

The story of Jesus' life is that all of us have our unique meaning. If we are born in a stable, unable to find accommodation, God will send shepherds to watch over us. If of uncertain parentage, God himself and Joseph will be our father. Sending wise men from the distant corners of the earth, to show that our one solitary life will still bless and influence the world.

And if we die forsaken on a cross, with no human or religious consolation, there is one at least who sends angels to open up our grave, bringing us out of our grave-clothes, and saying 'our living has not been in vain'.

As we get older we are like John the fisherman, the only disciple to grow old and lose his memory. He stretched out his arms to old age, and found himself bound with cords he did not wish, and taken to situations he never expected. In old age also, though we cannot sense it, God loves us and is our friend.

91

Do I exist, Lord?
    I am sure you do.
And because you exist, I exist also.
You are always thinking of me,
    always loving me.
Yet I wonder often,
    my mind eroded away
    by the world's neglect,
    no one saying thank-you,
    no one acknowledging my attempts to
        contribute.
I wonder how you feel, Lord.
    Much the same, I wouldn't wonder!

92

When my mother and father leave me,
    your love holds me up.
When my children grow up and leave
        home,
    your love protects them wherever
        they go.
Your love protects me also,
    surrounds me, enables me.
Lord, you are always with me.
    Till the world's end, and beyond.

93

Get a move on, Lord.
 No one else will.
Let your trumpets sound, for a change.
Let the walls of apathy and neglect
 come tumbling down.
I've walked about the city long enough.
 So have you, I imagine.
The trumpets are all ready in your hand.
 One, two, three . . .
  The count-down to your kingdom has
   begun!

94

It's all a trick, Lord.
I'll never get out of this world alive.
But you managed it.
In one moment of pure affection
 for my sake, you shouted
  'It is finished'.
So it is, Lord.
I am your work now.
 Your responsibility,
  as you are mine.

95

I thank you, Lord, for all the blessings of
  my life.
  Those souls I have been able to help.
  Those who have loved me.
  Those good things I was able to try,
    even if they did not turn out as I
      had planned,
    you had envisaged.
I fill my mind with your love, Lord.
  In all weathers you come to me,
  and are my friend.

96

Take me out of the pit, dear Lord.
  For your glory, not mine.
Raise me up,
  bind your love around me,
  uphold me, save me.
And if you cannot deliver me, Lord,
  from the pit,
  deliver me in it.
Come to me.
  Share my life.
    Uphold me.

97

As the deer longs for the water-brook,
    so does my soul long for you.
Even if one leg is broken, I come to you.
You wait for me, and give me your word.
As the eagle flies to your glory,
    so do I live.
Even if one wing is damaged,
        the currents of your love uphold me,
            bless me.
        I rest on your love.
As the fish in the sea,
    I make use of the currents,
        to swim to your glory.

98

Dear Lord, you are my shepherd.
Emperors count their subjects.
    Prime ministers their votes.
But you only count me your friend.
    Day by day you count me.
    You know me by name.
    Your love calls me, leads me on.
    Your flock is never complete

till I am inside.
While the Emperor shouts, 'Count
      everybody',
   you look at me and say,
      'My life is enough'.

99

I look at the stars, Lord,
   all the heavens and galaxies
   your love has created.
I feel so small beneath them,
   yet you have made them,
   for my sake.
I count the stars,
   stretching away beyond infinity.
But you count the possibilities of my life.
Your spirit come to me.
In all the stars in love's firmament,
   I have my special place,
      and shine to your glory.

100

Was it a case of mistaken identity, Lord?
We who took you for the gardener,
    up so early on the first day
        of the world's week,
    planting new seeds in our flower bed,
    so glad to see us,
    encouraging every sign of life,
        however small above the soil.
It is a new world again today, Lord,
    a new Eden.
And so, I do not think it was a case
    of mistaken identity,
        but of identity taken, and used
            to bless our souls forever.

101

Can a bad gardener
    be a good priest, Lord?
I don't know.
Only that you nourish my soul,
    and tend each plant in my garden.
Who knows to what size
    the smallest plant may grow?

102

The world gives me menus, Lord,
   but you give me food.
The world gives me diagnoses, assessment,
   lists of failures or strengths.
But you diagnose my true condition,
   you assess my true nature,
     that I am your friend forever.
You don't assess my soul's bank account,
     Lord.
   You add to it.

103

You found me a suitable case for treatment.
Leaving aside the white coat,
   and tools of your profession,
   you leaned over the doctor's desk,
   came round it,
     helped pull my boat up Galilee's beach.
Described the nets as the best you'd seen.
Looked at the blue sea, stretching away,
   and my day, opening in front of me.
You told me, I am just the person you
     need.

104

I serve you in fear, Lord.
Not in fear of you hurting me,
    but of me hurting you.
I set out on your journey.
I climb your mountain.
I respect the heights and depths
    this life has to offer.
Use the ropes and tackle available.
Breathing your air,
I fill my lungs with your goodness.
    I approach the summit.

105

We all say 'Amen', Lord, in our own way.
Each of us has our own place
    in that galaxy of human souls
        that shine to your glory.
I shine to your glory, Lord,
    not with my own light,
    but in my own way.
This day I give you glory.

106

Dear Lord, you are my rock.
   I build my house on you,
   this day on you.
With the materials you have given me.
Who am I to say,
   who is anyone to say,
   the materials you have given me are
      inadequate?
And if they are inadequate,
   that is only to stop me
   building taller houses than my
      neighbours'.
The weaker the material,
   the closer I will build to the ground.

107

It's not where I am now, Lord,
   that defines me,
   but where I am looking.
Not what I have now,
   but what I will have,
   what will possess me,
     in the future.

Lord, my eyes are fixed on you
   and on your kingdom,
   as your eyes are fixed,
   and your heart is fixed,
     on my welfare forever.

108

My bags are packed, Lord,
   I am ready to leave.
   I have sent on many of my attributes,
     except that one attribute
    you yourself have given me.
The less I have here on earth,
   the more there is waiting for me
    on the other side.
More friends, more mountains to climb,
   more paths to explore.
Meanwhile I cherish this last gift,
   and also the first you gave me.
I am always myself,
   and you give me meaning.

109

I am tired of being told, Lord,
  to lift up my heart.
  I want somewhere to put it down.
Foxes have holes, birds have nests,
  but we have nowhere to lay our heads,
    or our hearts,
    except in you, who travel with us.

110

You are Lord of my health, not of my
    sickness.
Yet you are Lord in my sickness.
  Leading my soul by your still waters.
    Feeding me,
    feeding my imagination.
Whatever things are of good report,
  helpful to me.
Whatever things are clean, lovely and
    helpful,
    clean, lovely and helpful to me,
    I think on these things.
    And lay my soul down to rest,
      by your river.

111

I set my troubled heart at rest,
    in your word, but also your silences.
Day by day I rest my soul
    in your refusal to judge me,
       refusal to leave me,
       refusal to write me off.
To you I am never redundant.
    Always essential, to your plans,
       to the world's blessing

112

I long for a big service, Lord.
    As Elijah did.
    Clergy, choirs, robes,
    the movement of vestments to solemn
       music.
But all you gave him is all you give us.
    A broken heart.
    A life that wished it had done better.
    An altar soaked in tears.
By your love
    it still shall catch fire.
'A broken and a contrite heart,
    you will not despise.'

113

Show me your spirit, Lord.
Let your star shine again.
   Leading us forward
   through the dark places
   to our journey's end.
      The end of this day.

114

Help us to look beyond the prayer-book,
      Lord.
   Beyond the prayers,
   beyond the hymns,
   to you who are the source of our life.
Help us to praise you in the morning.

115

Help me to remember the use of silence,
      Lord;
   my silence, not other people's.
Help me to pray for my friends, Lord.
   I meet them today.

They will make their journey
   to my life in their own time.
Help me to remember them
   when they have gone.
That will make their journey home safer.
Help me to be available to your needs in
    them.
   Now and always.

116

I tend to expect the worst, Lord.
   Usually I am right!
And if things do go well,
   I cannot feel it.
   But you can.
You know the value of my life.
Lift me up, then, in your love.
Let me forget all things,
   except your love for me,
     this tenderness.
Wrap your arms around me,
   clothe me in your love,
   and let my own mind be restored,
   in all these moments you have given me.

117

Dear Lord, I praise you.
  My praise is precious to you.
  My life matters.
Like the two sparrows sold for a farthing,
  my cries are heard
  along with all the praises
  of the great congregations.
My prayers rise up to you,
  you listen to me,
  and hear me gladly,
  and in my heart and voice,
    help me to pray.

118

Do you have a celibacy guidance bureau,
    Lord,
  for those who have difficulty,
  living with themselves?
I go to bed, and I am there.
  Still there in the morning,
  and on the farthest business-trip,
  all airports are the same, and so am I.

And yet, I am not the same to you,
  Day by day the light casts new shadows
    and nuances of love on my life.
Things not seen before,
  are noticed afresh by you.

119

Behold what manner of love the Father
    has shown us.
For you call us friends, Lord,
  not patients, cases, candidates.
And yet we are candidates for your love.
  Suitable cases for your treatment,
    of unbridled affection.
And yes, we are patient also,
  as we listen to your word,
    morning by morning.

120

In your law will I exercise myself, Lord.
  Gentle press-ups, and knees-bending,
    in the art of your love.
You who ask for our friendship,

not our success.
Our attempts at constancy,
    never our achievement.
You who love us,
    world without end,
    and beyond the world's end,
    without judgement.

121

Do you remember the phone, Lord?
    It used to be an intrusion.
    As I was going out, or staying in,
    working at that canvas
    you yourself had provided for that day.
But now it is silent
    and I have time to pray,
    thinking of one person a day,
        before I phone.
Two minutes on my knees.
    Twenty seconds.
Whoever does not begin by kneeling
        down
    runs every possible risk.

122

Help me not to dwell on the past, Lord.
I was happier then.
Or if not happier,
   had hopes of happiness,
   knew where I was,
   had some sense of my own identity,
     my place in the world,
     your plans for me.
No doubt I could never approach them.
   Who can?
   But I had some sense of 'belonging'.
But now I look back on these snapshots,
   people who were young when I was
      young,
   and have now arrived in the world,
   while I am lost,
     peering out from their daughters'
      weddings,
     members of the golf club,
     members of that human family
      from which I am barred.
Your spirit blesses them, Lord, through me.
You lift me up.
My childhood is safe somewhere.

You help me to unlatch my own blinds.
The light coming in is dull,
but part of a greater light
    shining on me, in your love.

123

The night is your territory also, Lord.
You are king in the dark hours also,
    though my soul does not see it.
You are my shepherd,
    watching over me in the darkness.
You know me by name.
    You love me.
    You call me to your service.
    You call me your friend.

124

Lord, you are the first person I talk to.
Before I talk to you,
    listen to your silences,
    I am in no state to talk with anyone else,
        or listen to you in them,
        your word in them.
            Amen.

125

I would have asked you back to earth,
    Lord,
    but my mind was somehow occupied
        with other things.
    The children's schooling,
    my own career,
    my family's prospects.
And yet we have no better prospect, Lord,
    than that of your return.
    No better schooling,
        than the learning of your love.
    No better career,
        than that of serving you.
In all of these things, Lord,
    you return daily.

126

I bear the burden
    and heat of the day, Lord.
    Your burden. Your day. Your heat.
I'd rather have a cheerful breeze,
    down from the seven hills
    that surround your city;

I understand that breezes are not made
    to order,
    blown to order.
They blow as they will;
    yet so does your good spirit,
    comforting me, refreshing me.

127

Why is it, Lord, that incurable diseases
    are so much easier to heal,
    than those of the mildly-indisposed?
Is it because my desperation
    opens a door to your kingdom
    others cannot find?
My life holds a key that turns the lock
    in a way never turned before?
Come then, Lord.
    You who are my door and home.

128

The main feature of Jesus' life was not that he
healed more people than anyone else. Though
his disciples, who had so misunderstood his

ministry at the time, liked to think, looking
back, that he had. In fact he healed those who
needed him, as he was able, or the Father was
able, in the one needing help. No doubt, in
this way, the few 'miracles' of love were like
the loaves and fishes, to influence the world.
But the main feature of Jesus' healing was not
the number healed, or the few who remained
with him to say 'thank you' or be 'evidence'.
The main and only feature of Jesus' ministry
was his love.

129

I've had this illness twelve years, Lord.
    For ages, then.
    I can't remember how long.
All right then, this illness has had me.
But though it has trapped me,
    it has never defined me.
I am your child,
    held by temporary chains.
The chains loosen,
    they are tired of seeming in control,
      but always knowing,

you are in control, Lord.
You the unchained one,
    who loosens my bonds.
You the chained one, who sings alleluia.

130

Familiarity breeds contempt. Sometimes it can also breed attempt, and the chance to follow Jesus more easily (more comfortably or securely), though life is never easy or comfortable.

Peter's fishing boat is also ours, with its place for Jesus' head to rest in the storm, and Andrew's lobster pots and the smell of varnish. Familiar things and prayers can help us as we grow older. Most of us come into the world hoping to be doctors, but end up being patients. As Jesus did, when he died in life's emergency ward, with two thieves or bandits in the beds on either side of him. Even then, though his arms were stretched out, and life had taken him where he had no wish to go, he found opportunity to bless others.

131

My life seems to be a history of mistakes,
   as all lives are.
Being human is a messy business, Lord,
   and your first disciples weren't saints,
   till they were dead.
In their lifetime they were messy saints.
You had to wash the smell of sea-weed
   out of their sandals.
Lord, help me to turn my sins to your glory.
One day I will be sinless and smiling,
   and possibly no use to anybody!
No one can stand a successful smiler!
But a failure, Lord, evokes sympathy.
His expressions for others' welfare
   enter the heart closely.
So Lord, I thank you in my sins,
   as you love me,
   one by one,
   my sins are blest by,
   received by,
   taken by,
      your love.

132

I have no need to shout, Lord.
The quietest whisper is enough.
The sound of our need
   is your opportunity.
The brokenness of our heart
   the only music needed.

133

Help me to say goodbye to the past, Lord.
   God be with you.
      Rest in peace.
The past is in your hands, Lord.
   It is never wasted.
Mistakes and virtues alike
   mingle beneath the soil,
      subside, in your own time, and theirs,
         plants will grow.
   Others will tend them,
      others pick your fruit.
Help me to say goodbye to the past, Lord.
   It is alive, in you.

134

Saying goodbye to the past is a great matter
and some people never manage it. Lot's wife
kept looking to the past and saying, 'Things
were not done like this in my grandfather's
day'. She became fixed, like a block of salt, or
a record stuck in its groove.

The children of Israel also looked to the
past. But it was memories pressed together
to become solid ground, on which to build
present lives. Not a sofa but a springboard. So
may our memories be.

135

You use parts of my soul I never knew
    existed, Lord.
Muscles I never knew I had
    had been exercised in my life by
        Galilee's beach.
But you took my boat from Galilee, Lord,
    out into the world,
      to catch your fish there,
      feed your people there.
Looking over the edge of my boat

into your deep waters,
I was conscious of my own littleness,
but of your love, above all.

136

The kingdom of heaven,
   your kingdom, Lord,
   is for the desperate,
   not the well-meaning.
It is for us
   desperate for your return,
   desperate in our own weakness,
   that makes us rely on your strength,
   your grace only.
Your love comes to us quickly,
     comes to us daily.

137

Help me to build your castle, Lord,
   not in the air, but on the ground.
   From the floor up.
   Foundations first.
   Walls in place.

Girders.
Cement to be mixed.
Here on the ground, Lord,
   beside your crib,
      I give you glory.

138

And would it have been the same, Lord,
   if you had retired to Tunbridge Wells
      and grown roses?
   Rejected by society,
   your church closing her doors,
   until your health collapsed,
      your mind broke,
      and nobody cared.
But we cared, Lord.
   In your nursing home we came to you.
   Listened to your broken mind reciting
      Galilee.
We bound you up.
   Rolled aside the stone from your life's
      sepulchre.
      And proclaimed: you are alive.

139

Help me to seek your glory, Lord,
   but also my own.
My own place in your kingdom
   no one else can fill.
My own calling, down by Galilee's shore,
   where I first met you, among the
      lobster pots.
Swiftly you come to my aid,
   now, as you did then.
You see me under the fig-tree,
   in the shadow of my own home.
You call to me.
   Your voice gives me meaning.

140

Help me to rest in your word, Lord.
   There is no need always to be
      speaking it.
Help me to rest in your love.
   There is no need always to be showing it.
Help me to rest in you,
   for if I do that, in your own time
      and my own,
      your word and your love will percolate
         outward.

FOR SINNERS ONLY

Jesus' religion, if he had one, was a religion for sinners. Peter and Paul were the chief exponents because they made most mistakes. 'Pray for all sinners of whom I am the chief' (Paul). Or, in Arabic terms, weave your mistakes into the fabric of your life. Do not always feel you have to unpick the threads. All lives are histories of errors and sins and missed opportunities, made opportune.

141

I'm not always as happy as I look, Lord.
  My mouth smiles, but my heart doesn't.
My heart is in pain, in darkness,
  while my mouth broadcasts kind
      messages,
    messages of hope I do not feel.
But you love me, Lord.
  You love to see me smile
  but love me in my anguish even more.
You are not a fair-weather friend.
When the shutters are down,
  and the wind blows, you come to me,
    and make my soul your home.

142

We have the power to hurt, Lord.
   You have only the power to be hurt.
Help me when I grow old, Lord.
   I am older today than yesterday.
Help me to see my helplessness
   as your opportunity.
      My weakness as your strength.

143

What do you mean,
   I'm not doing anything, Lord?
      I'm worrying!
    Is not that enough?
To feel the pains of the world,
   before the world itself notices them.
To feel my children's dangers,
   while they walk care-free.
One day, Lord, I shall walk
   carefree in your presence.
But till then I love you in darkness,
   and thank you for worrying about me.

144

I see the dark side of your face, Lord.
    I feel the dark side, love's absence,
    lack of purpose in my own life.
But you are my purpose, Lord,
    and my song.
You are also my memory,
    my strength, my future.
Help me to hold your hand, Lord.
    Even when I can't feel it.

145

We don't always get to die
    when we expect, Lord.
    A slow graceful exit,
    the world seeing, you seeing,
        what we have done.
But in the world's time
    we are broken and brought low,
        made ill and poor
        when we can ill afford it.
Our only comfort
    is that you, in darkness,
    are outside the camp also.

146

Help me to remember, Lord,
    death is not a failure to be alive.
    Sickness is not a failure to be well.
    This day we endure.
No, I am not my own master.
This condition I accept; no, I did not
       will it,
    and can only move forward
    at a snail's pace.
To be stationary, sometimes,
    is a great advancement.

147

Give me a prayer book, Lord,
    that will help me last till supper.
    However poor its pages,
    they will be well thumbed.
Till the prayer of need and emptiness
    and not being, not experiencing,
       is taken up into your darkness.
You live there, Lord, giving light to
       others.
    But have no sense of it yourself.

Star shining for me,
Star shining in me,
but not noticing,
never conscious of,
its own painful progress.

148

We don't always get the illnesses we
    choose, Lord.
  Sometimes they choose us.
  Coming on us suddenly, unawares.
This one condition we were not prepared
    for,
  helplessness, inability to choose
      another way.
Lord, I hold out my hands to you in
    helplessness,
  I cannot serve you now,
    only love you.
Yet this attention to your word
  is all you ever need
    to save the world through my
      weakness.

149

Help me, Lord, to use
    the life that I am given,
        in your way, my way,
        and no one else's.
The cards I am dealt
    no doubt could be better,
    but they provide, even the lower ones,
    some chance of contributing
        to the world's game.
Only you know the score, Lord.
Only you know who is winning,
    and at what.

150

Each life has its own meaning, Lord,
    though we often do not see it at the time.
Only at the end, journey completed,
    will I look back on my false steps,
        twisting footprints and see,
        even in the darkest times,
        how you were leading me,
        carrying me, walking beside me.

151

Help me to make the most of my life,
   Lord.
   The most of my death.
   This slow undressing of my powers.
Each life having a beginning, middle and
   end, Lord.
But only you know which order they
   come in.
   Which is my true 'end',
      my life's work,
      that soul for which I was created.
   Those lives for which I was put down
      on earth's entry list.
   So many years of tenure in another's
      property,
      until at last you call me home.

152

Some stones, Lord, cannot be moved.
Their massive solidity defies us.
   We cannot turn them to bread.
   Only live in their shadow.
   Walk around them,

build our lives on our own failures,
our own nothingness.
But you, Lord,
who see we have nothing,
love us,
remember how it was at our
beginning.
Helpless then, helpless now,
the world is still my cradle.

153

Help me to practise the faith, Lord.
I can't be expected to get the hang
of it.
Get the hang of your love for me,
which defies logic,
and yet has its own crazy inner
constancy.
That you love me always,
however I look,
whatever I do,
however I feel.

154

Help me to grasp the point of your life,
    Lord.
    Its point being that it has no point.
    Your agenda being that you have no
        agenda,
        beyond the agenda of my own life,
        my own happiness.
Dear Lord, work out your agenda in me.

155

Books about water, Lord, I don't need.
    I who am a fish in your sea.
Books about air are no help,
    to one who wishes only to fly in your sky.
Help me to fly, Lord,
    Resting on your love.
Help me swim in
    that ocean of your affection
        I can never see.
Hold it, Lord,
    I'm coming.
    As well as I can.
    One awkward step at a time.

156

Thank you, Lord,
   for knowing me
      better than I know myself.
   For loving me,
      more than I love myself.
   For forgiving me,
      more than I ever can begin to.
Thank you
   for believing in me,
      long after I gave up hope,
   for seeing my future,
      when I saw only darkness.
Thank you
   for being beyond the darkness,
      in the darkness,
      my friend.

157

Sinners only need apply.
I saw the notice, Lord,
   on your first church.
   Built of wood and straw,
      in Bethlehem.
The ox and ass,

your first congregation,
thinking to themselves
what good taste you showed
in calling them.
And so you call me
to another day.

158

Dear Lord,
I am one of those people
on the wrong side of life's road,
as the people pass me by
on the way to Jericho,
on their way from the holy city.
I try to make the journey
but find it too much for me.
Half dead and half alive,
I am only able to listen now and wait,
as well as I may,
for the sound of your donkey's footsteps.
Please stop, Lord,
as I know you always do.
Stop, pick me up,
carry me to safety.
It is your journey, Lord;
you make it with me.

159

Dear Lord, you know that the territorial
    instinct
  is for us humans the most basic
    instinct of all.
But what of us who have no territory,
  and no place to lay our head
  and call our own?
We are moved on.
  We have no chance
    to develop and grow.
But our roots are in you, Lord;
  the one without territory,
  without space,
  who yet gives us space
  to be ourselves,
  and is our territory
  and home for ever.

GROWING OLDER

When we are young, we set out on journeys to the empty tomb on Sunday morning, and get there first. We outrun Peter, who is older and short of breath. But when we are old, another in the form of old age or sickness binds us fast, and takes us where we have no wish to go. We are patients. Things happen to us. We do not apparently make them happen.

But in old age, or vulnerability and helplessness also, God is our friend. He watches over us and leads us, though we have no sense of his presence.

John the apostle was the only discile to know this. He lived to old age, looked back in love, and had arthritis.

160

Is there a life after Galilee, Lord?
I know I am getting older.
    All right, then, I have got old.
I feel young inside,
    but to others I seem older,
    and they laugh as I retell

the Galilee experience;
build a theme park of the time
when your catholic church
could get in a fishing boat.
Help me not to build theme parks, Lord,
but rest in your spirit,
carrying Galilee with me,
the true waves of your love
washing me clean.

161

Lord, I bless you in my weakness.
As the shadow of my life grows long.
And the list of people I have known,
places I have visited,
things I have done,
is longer than the list
of things, people, places
that are to be.
But I am myself, Lord.
As I was before I did anything,
went anywhere, met anybody.
I am myself, as I will be at the end.
Simply, your servant
whom you delight in.

162

We all die at different speeds, Lord.
    This slow undressing of our powers.
    Eyesight, hearing, teeth and hair
        falling out,
    our memory going.
Have I told you this before?
Or have you only told me one thing,
    all my life long.
    I am always your servant,
        in your good employment,
        as the day ends.

163

All sickness or old age is a 'taking of us where
we have no wish to go'. In old age and
breakdown we are God's friends also, and may
do more than we ever realise. We are always
indispensable to God. As we get older, the past
may be the only thing we have left. It is in
any case more secure. The blessings we have
helped others to, can never be taken away.
The sins we have committed can only be
forgiven.

There is no need to dwell on the past, except with love. Even if we are old and broken, the future belongs to us especially, as it does to the young.

Old age is a blessing, not a failure to be young. Love gathers up the fragments that remain that nothing be lost.

164

Youth is glorious, Lord,
   though it is not a career.
Old age has its honour too, Lord,
   though fewer people see it.
Fewer people, hardly any people,
   come up to my inadequate speech,
   and blurred memory, and uncertain
     vision,
    to congratulate me,
    to bless me for this weakness,
    as they did, years ago,
    when in my cot
    I was similarly disadvantaged.
But you see my disadvantage
   as your advantage, Lord.

You bless me.
After so many wounds and failures,
I still cling to you.
Lord, I thank you
  for what you have given me,
  for what you have taken away,
  for what you have left me.
    Amen.

165

I have started counting my Christmas
    cards, Lord.
  How much am I valued?
  How much am I worth?
As the cards get less, Lord,
  what used to be a nuisance
  cluttering up the mantelpiece,
  becomes a triumph.
I count each one lovingly.
  Fewer than last year.
  I am getting old.
Most of my friends are beside the crib
    now,
  not talking about it.

166

When I was young, Lord,
   I put my own clothes on, to some
      extent.
The clothes I was given,
   heredity and my own circumstances
      provided.
But now I am older, Lord,
   and I stretch out my arms,
   another, in sickness or breakdown,
      takes me where I have no wish to go.
I have no option,
   things happen to me.
   I used to make them happen.
In all of this, Lord,
   you walk beside me and smile,
   and say 'Well done!'
As well as I may
   I struggle to say your favourite word.
      Amen.
   There. I've managed it!
   May your kingdom come in my
      weakness now.
      So be it.

167

Each life has a beginning, Lord,
   a middle, and an end.
   But not necessarily in that order.
Help me to remember then,
   as I approach my closing years,
   enter them, endure them,
   this slow undressing of my powers.
Help me to know this only,
   my end is not necessarily
   the defining of my life.
My true conclusion may have come earlier,
   and be kept safe for me,
     as death approaches.
Nothing good, Lord, is ever lost,
   only deferred.

168

I am all alone, Lord.
My partner has died,
   the children have left home.
   And even if they have not,
     they have their own lives to lead,
     their own agendas,
    and I, who was once their stay and
       centre,

am no longer so essential,
except by my prayer,
to them.
Help me to remember, Lord,
as my life collapses,
that I am always essential to you.
You can manage the world, without me,
and have done so for some time.
But though you can manage, Lord,
I'm not sure you want to.

169

One difficulty of growing old is that no one else can see it happening. Only we can see ourselves, where inside we remain always fifteen or seventeen or twenty-five. Other people can only see the outside, and may be helpful in telling us how well we have already done. And pointing out that our broken mind or memory is only a sign of how much we have already borne, or been asked to remember.

Sometimes inactivity can be a blessing, though usually we need activity of a different sort. In old age or illness we still need to be needed. Our occupation is never gone. Only changed.

170

It is not easy repeating oneself, Lord,
     saying:
   'I love you,
   and I will follow you',
      for the second and third,
      for the three-hundredth time.
Yet we do it,
   as well as we can.
As a young man or woman first,
   more easily.
Then, when we are older
   and tied down to the world and life
   by a thousand little cords,
   we say again the old words:
   'Lord, you know that I am your friend.'
And though we say it with awkwardness,
   with rheumatism in our limbs
   and tiredness and lost opportunities in
      our hearts,
      still you hear us,
      and receive us,
      and lead us on.

171

When all hope is gone, Lord,
   you are born.
When the darkness is complete,
   you come.
When things are beyond despair,
   I find you.
You roll back the stone
   and are there to greet me.

NIGHT

Jesus of Nazareth left us his crucifixion. It was all he had to leave ultimately. His utter failure to convert the world, which was perhaps, in retrospect, better than other people's success in manipulating it.

But if Jesus only left his cross, Peter and Andrew at least left their fishing boat. Which is where Christians find comfort too. A lot of religious custom is to help people avoid too much crucifixion: too much reality. The smell of the varnish on Peter's boat, the rowlocks and oars in place, and Thomas' fishing net, are all comforts, like the prayers we say, to help us feel at home. That each of us has our own place in the boat. And our own contribution to the journey. It is important then to know where our waste paper basket is. To have places in the boat or on land where we can go to sleep, and not be disturbed. We need all the comfort we can get. Help to bear our own cross, and help with our burdens.

The problem always remains acute. Not whether God exists, but whether we do: and, if so, how?

172

The night comes, Lord,
   when no one can work.
Help me to remember you, Lord.
   Or if I cannot manage that,
   help me to know
   you do not forget me.
Those long sleepless nights,
   when I look over the edge of my life,
   and seem to have taken nothing.
     It is all in vain.
It is not in vain, Lord.
You come to me in the darkness,
   walking over the water.
You are on the edge of the shore,
   preparing my breakfast.

173

The night comes,
   when no one can work.
   Nor should we be expected to.
   The ending of any day
   or sport or activity,
     is not a failure on

>   my aching limbs' part,
>   my aching mind's.
> It is a chance to look back over the day,
>   what has gone before,
>   and rejoice in blessings given,
>   pray for blessings in situations left
>   empty.
> No one can do everything, Lord.
>   Not even you, all in one go.
> Lord, I bless you in the evening,
>   and do not regard it as 'a failed morning'.
>   Each hour, each moment,
>   has its glory.

174

> Out of the deep, I call to you, Lord.
> The deep anguish of things closes me
>   around.
>   There is no way out.
>   If there were, honourably, possibly,
>   you would have given it,
>   I might have taken it.
>   But now it seems too late.
> Bless my lost opportunities, Lord;

paths not taken, years ago.
They are not lost opportunities,
   only opportunity deferred.
A chance for you.

175

Jesus was asleep sometimes when he should have been awake. And awake when everyone else was resting. In the boat on Lake Galilee, with the waves rising higher and the wind roaring against the sails, Jesus slept with his head on a cushion. He could do nothing about the weather, and his disciples upbraided him for it. Later in the garden of Gethsemane he remained awake, to the human condition and his own betrayal, which was all he had left with which to bless the world and show goodwill. His disciples all slept then and were concerned he did not do the same.

May God bless us and help us to sleep, when we can do nothing about the weather. May he help us to be awake to betrayals no one else can see.

176

When I am awake at night,
 toiling in my imagination,
  catching nothing,
 you come to me over the water.
What cannot sustain me,
 what cannot sustain anyone,
  is enough to convey your love.

177

Help me to remember, Lord,
 you don't will my sufferings,
  though you do in a sense permit them.
You are the fount of my life,
 but are yourself constantly thwarted
  in your love of me.
You love me,
 but the world is dark.
You come to me,
 but I cannot feel you,
  cannot see you.
I am like the fish
 who did not believe in water.
Help me, Lord, to swim in you.

178

Thank you for my sleeplessness, Lord,
　　turning over in bed,
　　turning over the problems of the day.
　　They seem bigger, Lord,
　　they are bigger.
　　They weigh me down, but not out.
I wish I could sleep.
　　And yet, Lord,
　　this sleeplessness is your blessing.
　　You cannot sleep either,
　　　for all the sins of the world.
　　You lie awake,
　　you stand awake,
　　shepherd in my field, watching over.

179

My wife is sleeping soundly, Lord.
　　She shouldn't be.
Everyone else is sleeping soundly, except
　　you and me.
They don't know about the world,
　　obviously.
　　They are passing by on the other side.

Often the best place to be, Lord.
One eye on you.
One on your world.
Both eyes on the world, Lord,
in you, through you, only.

180

Death is not a worry to me, Lord,
though I am afraid of darkness,
afraid of dying.
Afraid of my own condemnation,
asking why I had not done better.
But you are greater than my heart, Lord.
You ask me, why I did not do worse.
You are pleased by my triumphs,
you see light in the darkest places of
my life.
In my greatest failures
you observe tiny fragments of virtue,
no one else had noticed.
You gather them up at the last day.
You say to me, 'Morning at last'.

181

I've done it, Lord,
   got to bed time.
The world ends tonight,
   and even if it doesn't,
      mine will, in one way or another.
Sometimes the evening comes early,
   and in the darkness I am conscious
      of nothing at all.
But you are conscious of me, Lord.
   You've always been my great believer.
   I hear your voice saying, over and over
         again,
   'It doesn't matter
      whether you believe in me, child.
   That depends on your make-up.
      I believe in you.'

182

Those who pray badly also sleep well, or
      deserve to.
Those who cannot pray at all are also
         your servants,
   doing as well as they can,
   with the faith they have,

the doubt they possess.
That also, no doubt, is your gift to them.
And so I lay my head on your pillow,
   unworried by my own lack of prayer or
      feeling.
You make up for it, Lord.
   You have enough faith for both of us.

183

Help me to hear the music of your life,
   Lord.
It is better to be born in ignominy,
   than to leave others
     outside in the stable.
Better to die in desolation
   without any comfort
   from man or religion,
   than to leave others
     similarly disadvantaged.
Better to rise again in our hearts,
   though your own life is broken and
      complete.
Better to come to life in others,
   that they and we
   may be blessed at the last.

184

I lie down to sleep and take my rest.
   But my mind doesn't rest.
   Someone has left the ignition on;
   it keeps racing round the garden.
Put your hand on the ignition, Lord.
   Slow the engine down quietly
      if you cannot switch it off.
Here I am, counting sheep now.
   They are jumping about in my head.
Can't you slow them down, Lord?
   You should be able to.
   You are their shepherd also.

185

Thank you Lord, for the places I did not
      go to,
   the friends I did not meet,
   the work I did not accept.
You went there but so did I,
   in my thought,
   your prayer in me.
Nothing, Lord is ever wasted.
   Nothing is lost.

186

Those who walk in darkness are part of a valued family. Which begins with a star shining brightly so that wise men can travel safely, though the star itself has no sense of its own light.

Jesus himself died in darkness, an outcast from his own society and religious tradition, and is still the great outsider. His lonely death on the cross, with its moment of utter dereliction, is seen as our point of atonement; when human nature is reduced to its utter aloneness in the solitude of each human life, which I hope may lead to the realisation that we are all uniquely loved.

187

Lord, you are always with me.
    No weakness can keep you away,
    no besetting sin.
In all seasons,
    at all times,
    you are with me,
    until we meet again
    in your kingdom.

300=